Water! Hot and Cool

CONTENTS

NATIONAL GEOGRAPHIC  Hampton-Brown

School Publishing

Words with Long <u>a</u>

Look at each picture. Read the words.

a_e

Example:

pl<u>a</u>t<u>e</u>

c<u>a</u>p<u>e</u>

l<u>a</u>k<u>e</u>

v<u>a</u>s<u>e</u>

sk<u>a</u>t<u>e</u>

c<u>a</u>k<u>e</u>

High Frequency Words

cold
drink
feel
form
live
three
turn
water

Key Words

Look at the pictures.
Read the sentences.

What Water Can Do

1. Water can **turn** into **three forms**.
   Match the forms to the pictures.
2. One form is very **cold**.
3. You can **drink** this form.
4. This form will **feel** hot.
5. You cannot **live** without **water**!

How do you use water?

Phonics Games

NGReach.com

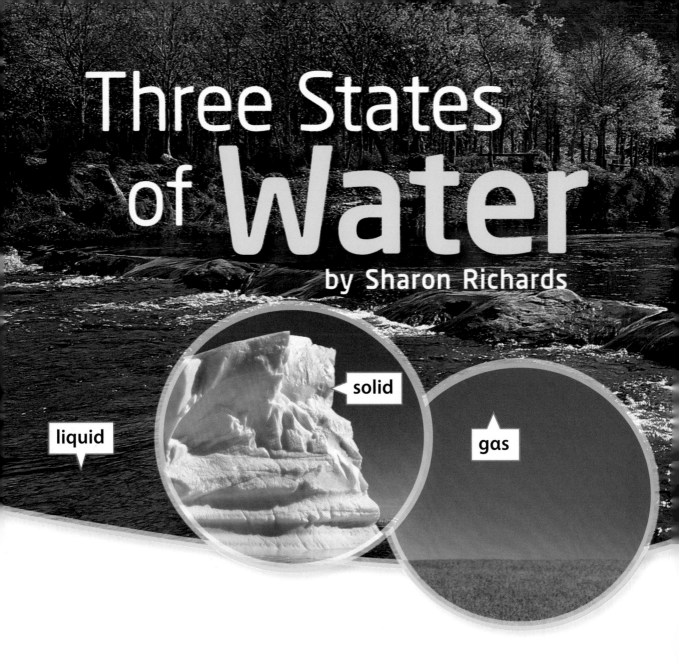

Three States of Water
by Sharon Richards

liquid

solid

gas

You know water. You drink it each day. But did you know that water has three forms, or states? It can be a liquid, a solid, or a gas.

When water gets very cold or hot, it
will not be in the same form. It will go
from one state to the other.

Liquid

Fill a glass with tap water. See how the water runs? It is in a liquid state. Water fills the shape of this glass.

rain

This is water as a liquid:
- You can see it drop as rain.
- You can drink it.
- You can swim in it.

Solid

Do you live in a cold spot? Look at a lake when it's very cold. You can't wade in it. Feel the top. You can scrape it. The water is solid.

This is water as a solid:
- You can skate on it.
- You can catch a big flake.
- You can drop it in a drink.

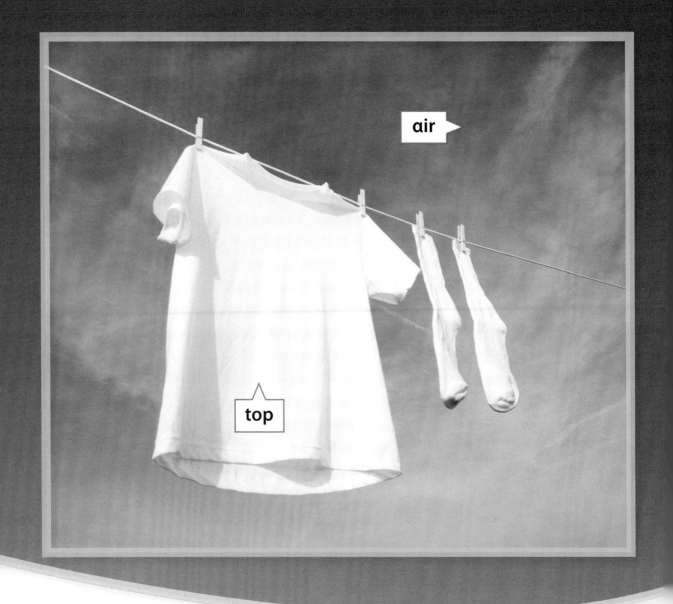

air

top

Gas

Hang up a wet top. Wait. Then come back and feel it. Is it still wet? No! The water turned from a liquid into a gas. The gas is in the air. You can not see water when it is a gas.

There is water in the air:
- This water is a gas
- You can not see it.

Can you name each state of water?
When it's in this state, you can wade in it.

When it's in this state, you can skate
on it.

When it's in this state, you can not see it. But in all states, it's still water. ❖

Words with Long <u>a</u>

Read these words.

game	wish	take	cake
sip	vase	fill	bake

Find the words with long **a**.
Use letters to build them.

g   a   m   e

Talk Together

Choose words from the box
to tell your partner what the
children might say they can do
with water.

I can _bake_ a _cake_.

1.

2.

3.

Syllables

Look at each picture. Read the words.

Example:

cupcake
▲

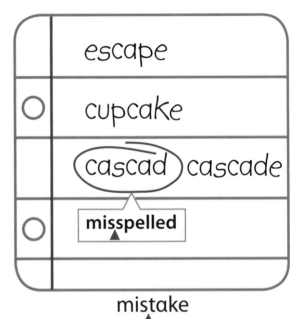

escape

○ cupcake

(cascad) cascade

○ **misspelled**
▲

mistake
▲

escape
▲

cascade
▲

unmade bed
▲

High Frequency
Words

| cold |
| drink |
| feel |
| form |
| three |
| turn |
| live |
| water |

Key Words

Look at the picture. Read the sentences.

Drinks for Pals

1. We cannot **live** without **water**.
2. **Turn** on the tap.
3. In this **form**, you can **feel** the water rush out.
4. Get a **drink** of **cold** water.
5. Fill **three** cups for your pals, too.

Why is it good to drink water?

Phonics Games

NGReach.com

17

Water
Is Important

by Carl Murano

There is one thing you must take each day.
It's unsafe not to take it. Think a bit. What is it?
It's water!

Why is water important? We can't live
without it. All life forms must get water.

You can't tell, but 60% of your body is made up of water. Yes, 60%! That's not a mistake. But water goes out of your body each day.

sweat

When you get hot, you sweat. When you sweat, your body gets rid of water. Also when you exhale (take a breath), your body gets rid of water. Can you get it back?

Yes! You can drink water. You can drink milk. You can eat things with lots of water inside, such as grapes and plums. Grapes and plums are filled with water.

It's a mistake to feel thirsty and not get water. It's unsafe! So grab a drink of cold water. Munch on things with lots of water inside.

How can we use water?

• We can take a bath in it.

• We can drink it.

• We can rinse with it.

- We can take a trip on it.
- We can water plants and grass.
- We can swim in it.

We use all this water without thinking.
It adds up. It is a shame how much water
we waste.

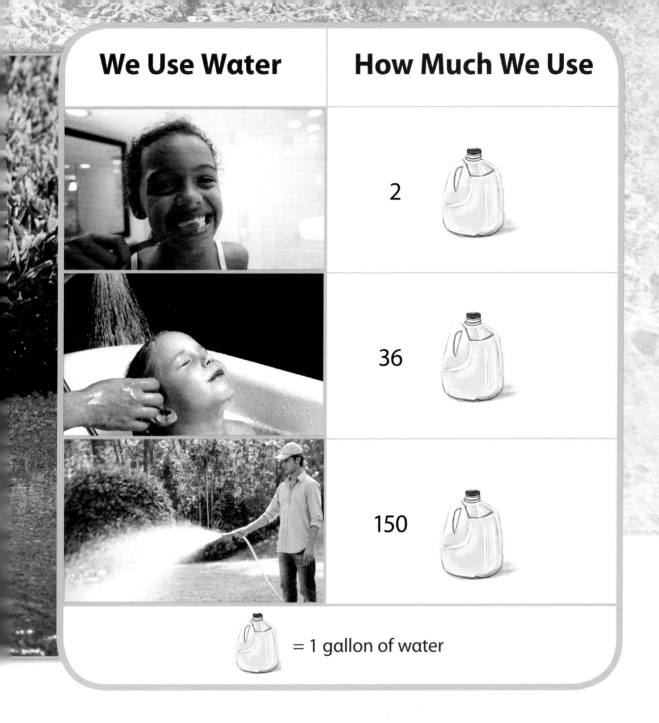

We Use Water	How Much We Use
	2
	36
	150

= 1 gallon of water

Think of things you do that take water.
See how much water it takes to do these
three things?

Thirsty? Turn on the tap and take a drink.
But don't be careless. Don't waste it! ❖

Syllables

Read these words.

forms	mistake	cupcake	drinks
milkshake	escape	makes	exhale

Find the words with two syllables.
Use letters to build them.

m   i   s   t   a   k   e

Talk **Together**

Choose words from the box
to tell your partner about
how Haldane uses water.

Haldane __makes__
a __cupcake__.

1.

2.

3.

Search and Find

Look at the picture with a partner. Take turns reading the clues and finding the answers.

1. A cascade fills the lake.
   Find the cascade.
2. It is unsafe to be in the sun too long.
   Find three spots to escape from the sun.
3. Jane takes her turn rinsing the plates.
   Find her.
4. Dave inflates a raft. Find him.
5. Mom feels a chill as she wades
   in the water. Find her.
6. Trish takes a cold drink. Find her.
7. Dad makes a mistake with the logs.
   Find him.

Acknowledgments
Grateful acknowledgment is given to the authors, artists, photographers, museums, publishers, and agents for permission to reprint copyrighted material. Every effort has been made to secure the appropriate permission. If any omissions have been made or if corrections are required, please contact the Publisher.

Photographic Credits
CVR Michael Quinton/Minden Pictures/National Geographic Image Collection. **2** (bcr, br) Photodisc/ Getty Images. (bl) Comstock Images/Jupiterimages. (cl) Eyewire. (tcr) Blend Images. (tl) Premier Edition Image Library/Superstock. **3** (b) Liz Garza Williams/Hampton-Brown/National Geographic School Publishing. (tc) John Foxx Images/Imagestate. (tl) Sebastian Duda/Shutterstock. (tr) Marvin Dembinsky Photo Associates/Alamy Images. **4** (l) Brand X Pictures/Jupiterimages. (r) thumb/ Shutterstock. **4-5** (bg) Stockbyte/Getty Images. **5** (inset) Alaska Stock LLC/Alamy Images. **6** HBSS/Corbis. **7** (b) PhotoDisc/Getty Images. (bg) Bruce Heinemann/PhotoDisc/Getty Images. (tl) Monkey Business Images/Shutterstock. (tr) Kristin Stith/Getty Images. **8** bbbb/Shutterstock. **9** (b, t) iStockphoto. (bg) Lorraine Swanson/Shutterstock. **10** (inset) Mike Flippo/Shutterstock. **10-11** (t) Kativ/iStockphoto. **12** Ajax/Zefa/Corbis. **13** LWA/Dann Tardif/Blend Images. **14** Carly Rose Hennigan/Shutterstock. **15** Liz Garza Williams/Hampton-Brown/National Geographic School Publishing. **16** (bl) Matthew Capowski/iStockphoto. (cl) Corey Hochachka/Design Pics Inc./Alamy Images. (r) DigitalStock/Corbis. (tl) Ruth Black/Shutterstock. **17** Liz Garza Williams/Hampton-Brown/National Geographic School Publishing. **18** (inset) BananaStock/Jupiterimages. **18-19** (bg) PhotoDisc/Getty Images. **19** (bl) Victor Prikhodko/iStockphoto. (br) STOCK4B/Getty Images. (t) Jeremy Woodhouse/PhotoDisc/Getty Images. **20-21** (bg) PhotoDisc/Getty Images. **21** (inset) Blend Images/Alamy Images. **22** (bl) Stockbyte/Alamy Images. (br, tl) Artville. (tr) Ljupco/iStockphoto. **22-23** PhotoDisc/Getty Images. **23** (inset) tracy tucker/iStockphoto. **24** (bl) oytun karadayi/ iStockphoto. (r) Juriah Mosin/Shutterstock. (tl) Stockbyte/Getty Images. **24-25** (bg) PhotoDisc/Getty Images. **25** (bl) Miroslav Ferkuniak/iStockphoto. (r) Corbis Super RF/Alamy Images. (tl) iStockphoto. **26-27** (bg) PhotoDisc/Getty Images. (inset) JoSon/Jupiterimages. **27** (b) Frederic Cirou/PhotoAlto/ Alamy Images. (c) PhotoDisc/Getty Images. (t) Blend Images/age fotostock. **28** (bg) PhotoDisc/Getty Images. (inset) Jason van der Valk/iStockphoto. **29** Liz Garza Williams/Hampton-Brown/National Geographic School Publishing.

Illustrator Credits
15, **17**, **20**, **27**, **29**, **30-31** Colleen Madden

The National Geographic Society
John M. Fahey, Jr., President & Chief Executive Officer
Gilbert M. Grosvenor, Chairman of the Board

National Geographic School Publishing
Hampton-Brown
www.NGSP.com

Printed in the USA.
RR Donnelley, Jefferson City, MO

ISBN:978-0-7362-8064-8

13 14 15 16 17 18 19
10 9 8 7 6 5